HOLLYWOOD FILM QUIPS

SPOKEN BY THE STARS

Compiled by
Susan Teltser-Schwarz

Design by
Michel Design

PETER PAUPER PRESS, INC.
WHITE PLAINS • NEW YORK

With thanks to John Biers

Contents

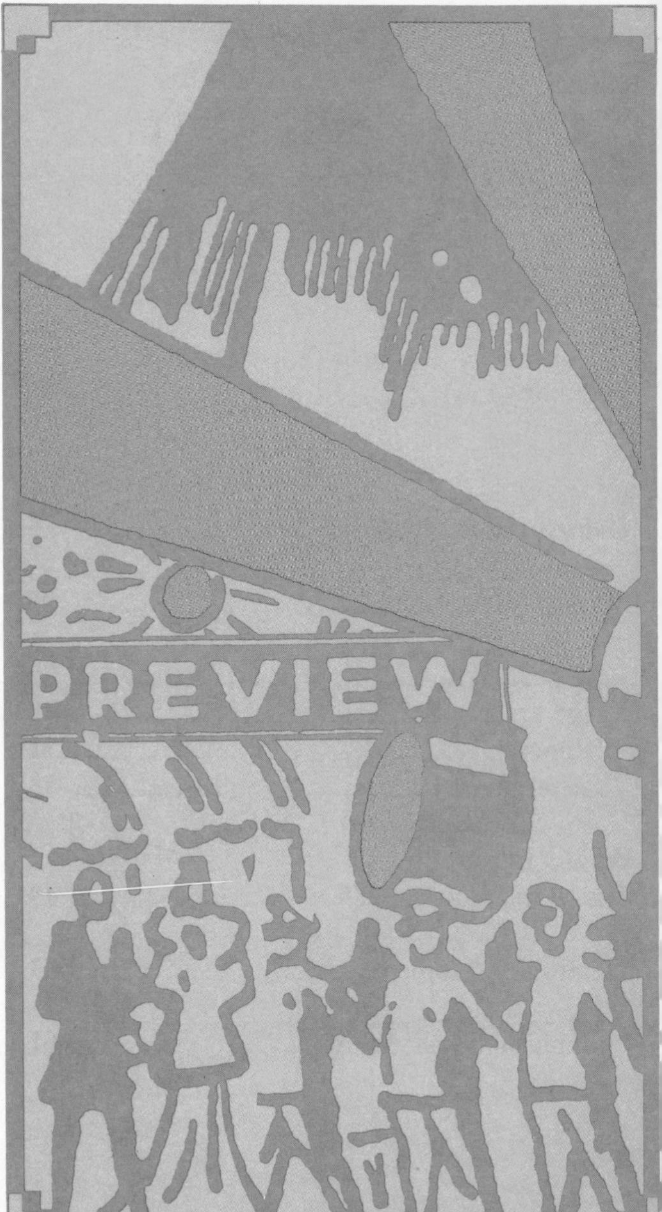
PREVIEW

UNFORGETTABLE LINES

Fasten your seat belts. It's going to be a bumpy night.

> BETTE DAVIS,
> *All About Eve*

Here's looking at you, kid.

> HUMPHREY BOGART,
> *Casablanca*

It's not the men in your life that counts, it's the life in your men.

> MAE WEST,
> *I'm No Angel*

Damn the torpedoes! Full speed ahead!

> CHARLES COBURN,
> *The More the Merrier*

We'll make him an offer he can't refuse.

MARLON BRANDO,
The Godfather

It is widely held that too much wine will dull a man's desires. Indeed it will—in a dull man.

NARRATOR,
Tom Jones

I can feel the hot blood pounding through your varicose veins.

JIMMY DURANTE,
The Man Who Came to Dinner

. . . people coming, people going—always coming and going and nothing ever happens.

LEWIS STONE,
Grand Hotel

With enough courage, you can do without a reputation.

CLARK GABLE,
Gone With the Wind

He's alive but unconscious, just like Gerald Ford.

from *Airplane*

Love means never having to say you're sorry.

RYAN O'NEAL,
Love Story

You should have seen me on the road to Morocco, but some overage crooner with laryngitis crabbed my act.

BOB HOPE,
The Princess and the Pirate

Why don't you get out of that wet coat and into a dry martini?

ROBERT BENCHLEY,
The Major and the Minor

May the Force be with you.

ALEC GUINNESS,
Star Wars

I'm still big. It's the pictures that got small.

GLORIA SWANSON,
Sunset Boulevard

We didn't need dialogue, we had faces.

GLORIA SWANSON,
Sunset Boulevard

... but, first and foremost, I remember
Mama.

BARBARA BEL GEDDES,
I Remember Mama

You don't understand . . . every night when
the moon is full, I turn into a wolf.

LON CHANEY,
Abbott and Costello Meet Frankenstein

She came at me in sections.

FRED ASTAIRE,
The Band Wagon

Your idea of fidelity is not having more
than one man in bed at the same time.

DIRK BOGARDE,
Darling

If you want anything, just whistle.... You know how to whistle, don't you, Steve? You just put your lips together ... and blow.

LAUREN BACALL,
To Have and Have Not

Insanity runs in my family. It practically gallops.

CARY GRANT,
Arsenic and Old Lace

Is there a doctor in the house?

W. C. FIELDS,
Tillie and Gus

Come back, Shane!

BRANDEN DE WILDE,
Shane

That son of a bitch stole my watch!

ADOLPHE MENJOU,
The Front Page

My mother thanks you. My father thanks
you. My sister thanks you. And I thank
you.

JAMES CAGNEY,
Yankee Doodle Dandy

You played it for her, you can play it for
me. If she can stand it, I can. Play it!

HUMPHREY BOGART,
Casablanca

It's been four years since I saw you,
Sorrowful, but I recognize the suit.

LUCILLE BALL,
Sorrowful Jones

Frankly, my dear, I don't give a damn.
CLARK GABLE,
Gone With the Wind

Don't you think it's better for a girl to be
preoccupied with sex than occupied?
MAGGIE MCNAMARA,
The Moon Is Blue

I have heard of the arrogant male in
capitalistic society. Your type will soon be
extinct.
GRETA GARBO,
Ninotchka

Every man carries in his heart a Shangri-
La.
SAM JAFFE,
Lost Horizon

This is Sorrowful Jones, who fell in love
with money at the age of six, and they've
been going steady ever since.

WALTER WINCHELL, (NARRATOR),
Sorrowful Jones

You dog, you dirty yellow dog, you! You
ain't no son of mine!

MARJORIE MAIN,
Dead End

I killed a guy for looking at me the way you
are now.

HUMPHREY BOGART,
Dead End

What's up, Doc? . . . Of course you realize
this means war.

BUGS BUNNY,
Cartoon Character

You just gotta save Christianity, Richard!
You gotta!

Loretta Young,
The Crusades

I caught this guy stealing our water. Next
time you try that, I'll let it out of you
through little round holes.

Humphrey Bogart,
The Treasure of the Sierra Madre

It is a far, far better thing I do than I have
ever done. It is a far, far better rest I go to
than I have ever known.

Ronald Colman,
A Tale of Two Cities

Perhaps it's better if I live in your heart,
where you can't see me.

Greta Garbo,
Camille

Time marches on!

WESTBROOK VON VOORHIS (NARRATOR),
The March of Time (monthly newsreel)

You know, it takes two to get one in trouble.

MAE WEST,
She Done Him Wrong

We have ways of making men talk.

DOUGLASS DUMBRILLE,
Lives of a Bengal Lancer

I don't mind being drafted, but not for ammunition.

BOB HOPE,
The Road to Zanzibar

Why don't you come up sometime . . . see me?

MAE WEST,
She Done Him Wrong

Very stupid to kill the only servant in the house. Now we don't even know where to find the marmalade.

JUDITH ANDERSON,
And Then There Were None

Wait a minute, wait a minute, you ain't heard nothin' yet, folks!

AL JOLSON,
The Jazz Singer

Make my day!

CLINT EASTWOOD,
Sudden Impact

Whoever is bitten by a werewolf and lives
becomes a werewolf himself.

A GYPSY,
The Wolf Man

I am Dra-cu-la.

BELA LUGOSI,
Dracula

I have one word for you, Benjamin—
plastics.

WILLIAM DANIELS,
The Graduate

Do you know I read somewhere that
machinery is going to take the place of
every profession?

JEAN HARLOW,
Dinner at Eight

Me Tarzan, you Jane.

JOHNNY WEISSMULLER,
Tarzan the Ape Man

Cry? I never knew a woman that size had
that much water in her.

TONY RANDALL,
Pillow Talk

Excuse me while I slip into something
more comfortable.

JEAN HARLOW,
Hell's Angels

Remember, men, we're fighting for this
woman's honor . . . which is probably more
than she ever did!

GROUCHO MARX,
Duck Soup

I've met a lot of hard-boiled eggs in my time, but you—you're twenty minutes!

JAN STERLING,
Ace in the Hole

We've become a race of Peeping Toms. What people ought to do is get outside their own house and look in for a change.

THELMA RITTER,
Rear Window

If I ever go looking for my heart's desire again, I won't look any further than my own back yard because if it isn't there, I never really lost it to begin with.

JUDY GARLAND,
The Wizard of Oz

There ain't much meat on her but what there is is cherce.

SPENCER TRACY,
Pat and Mike

We all go a little mad sometimes.
ANTHONY PERKINS,
Psycho

Murder is a crime for most men, but a
privilege for the few.
JAMES STEWART,
Rope

It's a funny old world—a man's lucky if he
can get out of it alive.
W. C. FIELDS,
You're Telling Me

Either this man is dead or my watch has
stopped.
GROUCHO MARX,
A Day at the Races

. . . one of my most precious treasures . . . is
an exquisite pair of loaded dice, bearing
the date of my graduation from high
school.

> W. C. FIELDS,
> *Let's Look at the Record*

What's a thousand dollars? Mere chicken
feed. A poultry matter.

> GROUCHO MARX,
> *The Cocoanuts*

Look at me: I worked my way up from
nothing to a state of extreme poverty.

> GROUCHO MARX,
> *Monkey Business*

Well, I guess I've done murder. Well, I guess
I won't think about that. I'll think about
that tomorrow.

> VIVIEN LEIGH,
> *Gone With the Wind*

There comes a time in the affairs of men, my dear Blubber, when we must take the bull by the tail and face the situation.

W. C. FIELDS,
Tillie and Gus

Don't forget Lady Godiva put everything she had on a horse.

W. C. FIELDS,
Tillie and Gus

I didn't squawk about the steak, dear. I merely said I didn't see that old horse that used to be tethered outside here.

W. C. FIELDS,
Never Give a Sucker an Even Break

Don't be too sure I'm as crooked as I'm supposed to be.

HUMPHREY BOGART,
The Maltese Falcon

Beulah, peel me a grape.

MAE WEST,
I'm No Angel

The calla lilies are in bloom again.

KATHARINE HEPBURN,
Stage Door

Shut up and deal.

JACK LEMMON,
Mister Roberts

After all, tomorrow is another day.

VIVIEN LEIGH,
Gone With the Wind

Th—that's all, folks!

MEL BLANC'S PORKY PIG VOICE,
What's Up, Doc?

SPOKEN BY THE STARS

Sex

Acting is like sex. You should do it and not talk about it.

JOANNE WOODWARD

The difference between sex and death is that with death you can do it alone and no one is going to make fun of you.

WOODY ALLEN

Thank God I'm in love again. Now I can do it for love and not my complexion.

JOAN CRAWFORD

He gives her class and she gives him sex.

KATHARINE HEPBURN,
on Fred Astaire and Ginger Rogers

I'm glad you like my Catherine. I like her too. She ruled thirty million people and had three thousand lovers. I do the best I can in two hours.

MAE WEST,
on her performance in
Catherine the Great

Here, I think this is what you want.

JUDY HOLLIDAY,
handing her falsies to a studio head
who was chasing her around the room

It (sex) was the most fun I ever had without laughing.

WOODY ALLEN

Personally I know nothing about sex because I've always been married.

ZSA ZSA GABOR

I am not a sexy pot.

SOPHIA LOREN

Lana Turner is to an evening gown what
Frank Lloyd Wright is to a pile of lumber.

REX HARRISON

Love is the answer, but while you are
waiting for the answer, sex raises some
pretty good questions.

WOODY ALLEN

I never slept with a man I wasn't married
to. How many women can make that
claim?

ELIZABETH TAYLOR

I like to wake up feeling a new man.

JEAN HARLOW

The important thing in acting is to be able to laugh and cry. If I have to cry, I think of my sex life. If I have to laugh, I think of my sex life.

GLENDA JACKSON

It's the kissiest business in the world. You *have* to keep kissing people.

AVA GARDNER

Age

I am just turning forty and taking my time
about it.

HAROLD LLOYD,
at age 77

A man's only as old as the woman he feels.

GROUCHO MARX

I prefer old age to the alternative.

MAURICE CHEVALIER

There are no old men any more. *Playboy*
and *Penthouse* have between them made an
ideal of eternal adolescence, sunburnt and
saunaed, with the grey dorianed out of it.

PETER USTINOV

She'll never admit it, but I believe it is
Mama.

ZSA ZSA GABOR,
when asked which Gabor
woman was the oldest

The toughest role is learning to grow up.

ELIZABETH TAYLOR

Money

I want a man who's kind and understanding. Is that too much to ask of a millionaire?

ZSA ZSA GABOR

I feel like a million tonight—but one at a time.

MAE WEST

There were times my pants were so thin I could sit on a dime and tell if it was heads or tales.

SPENCER TRACY

Money can't buy friends, but you can get a better class of enemy.

SPIKE MILLIGAN

Three things help me get through life
successfully—an understanding husband,
an extremely good analyst and millions
and millions of dollars.

MARY TYLER MOORE

My problem lies in reconciling my gross
habits with my net income.

ERROL FLYNN

General

It's lonely and cold on top.

JUDY GARLAND

When people say she's got everything, I've only one answer: I haven't had tomorrow.

ELIZABETH TAYLOR

A man in the house is worth two in the street.

MAE WEST

Thanks to the movies, gunfire has always sounded unreal to me, even when being fired at.

PETER USTINOV

Too much of a good thing can be
wonderful.

MAE WEST

An actor's a guy who, if you ain't talking
about him, ain't listening.

MARLON BRANDO

I never drink anything stronger than gin
before breakfast.

W. C. FIELDS

Somewhere behind every cloud, there's a
lot of rain.

JUDY GARLAND

Egotism—usually just a case of mistaken nonentity.

BARBARA STANWYCK

Imagine their delighted surprise when I read them the script of *Love and Death,* with its plot that went from war to political assassination, ending with the death of its hero caused by a cruel trick of God. Never having witnessed eight film executives go into cardiac arrest simultaneously, I was quite amused.

WOODY ALLEN

This is a free country, madam. We have a right to share your privacy in a public place.

PETER USTINOV

Acting is all about honesty. If you can fake that, you've got it made.

GEORGE BURNS

I just want to be normally insane. . . . I
agree that no man is an island, but I also
feel that conformity breeds mediocrity.

MARLON BRANDO

Many a man owes his success to his first
wife and his second wife to his success.

JIM BACKUS

Actually, it only takes one drink to get me
loaded. Trouble is, I can't remember if it's
the thirteenth or fourteenth.

GEORGE BURNS

Cocaine is God's way of saying you're
making too much money.

ROBIN WILLIAMS

An amateur thinks it's funny if you dress a man up as an old lady, put him in a wheelchair, and give the wheelchair a push that sends it spinning down a slope towards a stone wall. For a pro, it's got to be a real old lady.

GROUCHO MARX

The Academy asks that your speech be no longer than the movie itself.

DANNY KAYE

Marlon Brando and I have a lot in common. He, too, has made many enemies.

BETTE DAVIS

You can lead actresses to water and drink, but you can't make them wear what they don't want to.

EDITH HEAD,
costume designer

I made the mistake early in my career, when I moved to Hollywood, of being attracted to actresses. I used to go out exclusively with actresses and all other female impersonators.

MORT SAHL

Man made civilization in order to impress his girlfriends.

ORSON WELLES

Hey, now, listen, if actors have to work nude, and they're embarrassed about it, it should be union rules that the crew be nude, too, and then nobody will be staring at anybody.

JACK NICHOLSON

A world in which people cannot laugh isn't worth saving.

CHARLIE CHAPLIN

Success to me is having ten honeydew
melons and eating only the top half of each
one.

BARBRA STREISAND

What a holler would ensue if people had to
pay the minister as much to marry them as
they have to pay a lawyer to get them a
divorce.

CLARE TREVOR

When a woman behaves like a man, why
doesn't she behave like a nice man?

EDITH EVANS

Fighting is essentially a masculine idea: a
woman's weapon is her tongue.

HERMIONE GINGOLD

If at first you don't succeed, try, try again.
Then give up. No use being a damn fool
about it.

W. C. FIELDS

There is nothing an actor hates more than
the sound of people coming in while the
play is in progress—unless it's the sound of
people going out.

RONALD REAGAN

I don't care what is written about me as
long as it isn't true.

KATHARINE HEPBURN

Not only is God dead, but try getting a
plumber on weekends.

WOODY ALLEN

My movies were the kind they show in prisons and airplanes, because nobody can leave.

BURT REYNOLDS

Ah, stardom. They put your name on a star in the sidewalk on Hollywood Boulevard and you walk down and find a pile of dog manure on it. That tells the whole story, baby.

LEE MARVIN

Tragedy is if I cut my finger. Comedy is if I walk into an open sewer and die.

MEL BROOKS

The art of acting consists in keeping people from coughing.

RALPH RICHARDSON

Hollywood: A place where they shoot too many pictures and not enough actors.

WALTER WINCHELL

There's no way I'm going to risk having my real beauty—my voice—changed by a nose operation. If that happened, I'd be just another pretty face.

BARBRA STREISAND

Marilyn Monroe was all woman. She had curves in places other women don't even have places.

CYBILL SHEPHERD

You mean apart from my own?

ZSA ZSA GABOR,
on being asked how many
husbands she had had

When I did my first love scene, the director told me to use a longing expression, so I thought of a big, tender, rare steak.

CLARK GABLE

You can't find closeness in Hollywood. Everyone does the fake closeness so well.

CARRIE FISHER

Having the critics praise you is like having the hangman say you've got a pretty neck.

ELI WALLACH

Acting is the most minor of gifts and not a very high-class way to earn a living. After all, Shirley Temple could do it at the age of four.

KATHARINE HEPBURN

Everything you see I owe to spaghetti.

SOPHIA LOREN

They used to photograph Shirley Temple
through gauze. They should photograph
me through linoleum.

TALLULAH BANKHEAD

It was a woman who drove me to drink and
I never had the decency to thank her.

W. C. FIELDS

When I'm good, I'm very good, but when
I'm bad, I'm better.

MAE WEST,
I'm No Angel

Hindsight is always 20/20.

BILLY WILDER

Johnny, keep it out of focus. I want to win
the foreign picture award.

BILLY WILDER,
to his cinematographer,
while filming Sunset Boulevard

I was born at the age of twelve on a Metro-
Goldwyn-Mayer lot.

JUDY GARLAND

If my film makes one more person
miserable, I've done my job.

WOODY ALLEN

A successful man is one who makes more money than his wife can spend. A successful woman is one who can find such a man.

LANA TURNER

Please accept my resignation. I don't care to belong to a club that will have me as a member.

GROUCHO MARX

It's the good girls who keep diaries; the bad girls never have the time.

TALLULAH BANKHEAD

To err is human—but it feels divine.

MAE WEST

Hollywood is a great place if you're an orange.

FRED ALLEN

WHAT'S IN A NAME?
The Stars, Now And Then

Ray Milland	Reginald Truscott-Jones
Boris Karloff	William Henry Pratt
Robert Taylor	Spangler Arlington Brugh
Jennifer Jones	Phyllis Isley
Gene Wilder	Jerome Silberman
Danny Thomas	Amos Jacobs
Conway Twitty	Harold Lloyd Jenkins
Clifton Webb	Webb Parmalee Hollenbeck
Mario Lanza	Alfredo Cocozza
Doris Day	Doris von Koppelhoff
Greta Garbo	Greta Gustafsson

Ellen Burstyn	Edna Gilhooley
Alan Alda	Alphonso D'Abruzzo
Stan Laurel	Arthur Jefferson
Shelly Winters	Shirley Schrift
Jack Benny	Benjamin Kubelsky
Lauren Bacall	Betty Joan Perske
Dorothy Lamour	Mary Kaumeyer
Veronica Lake	Constance Ockleman
W. C. Fields	William Claude Dukenfield
Judy Garland	Frances Ethel Gumm
Rita Hayworth	Margarita Cansino
Kirk Douglas	Iussur Danielovitch Demsky
Judy Holliday	Judith Tuvim
Roy Rogers	Leonard Slye
Gypsy Rose Lee	Rose Louise Hovick
Michael Keaton	Michael Douglas
Steve Lawence	Sidney Leibowitz

Lillian Russell	Helen Leonard
Ted Knight	Tadeus Wladyslaw Konopka
Janet Leigh	Jeanette Morrison
Carole Lombard	Jane Peters
Mickey Rooney	Joe Yule, Jr.
Howard Keel	Howard Leek
Peter Lorre	Laszlo Lowenstein
Jerry Lewis	Joseph Levitch
Jane Wyman	Sarah Jane Fulks

MEMORABLE MOMENTS

When Shirley Temple was taken by her mother for a pre-Christmas visit to a department store Santa Claus, he asked for her autograph. That was the end of her belief in Santa.

Tallulah Bankhead appeared naked in Donald Sutherland's dressing room, and asked the startled actor:

What's the matter, darling? Haven't you ever seen a blonde before?

Asked if he liked children, W. C. Fields replied:

Only if they are properly cooked.

Ilka Chase, after her divorce from Louis Calhern, found some leftover "Mrs. Louis Calhern" calling cards and sent them on to his next wife with this note:

Dear Julia, I hope these reach you in time.

When Mae West was casting the leading man for She Done Him Wrong, *she took a look at Cary Grant and said:*

If he can talk, I'll take him.

A conversation between a Customs official and Alfred Hitchcock:

What do you produce?
—Gooseflesh.

In a scene for one of the Hope/Crosby/Lamour comedies, Dorothy Lamour dropped her sarong for a swim just as a passing train obscured her from view. In character, Bob Hope said:

I've been to see the picture eight times now and I'm going again. Sooner or later that train is bound to be late.

Greta Garbo spoke some memorable lines in her first sound movie, Annie Christie:

Gif me a visky, ginger ale on the side—and don't be stingy, baby.

About a rumor that she had died, Bette Davis said:

With the newspaper strike on I wouldn't consider it.

Eddie Cantor urged Jimmy Durante to be more than a piano player on the vaudeville stage:

People like you a whole lot. So why don't you get up on the floor and say something to the people? Make remarks while you're playing the piano?
—Gee, Eddy, I couldn't do that. I'd be afraid people would laugh at me.

Gregory Ratoff directed Ingrid Bergman this way:

Vy don' you spik English? Say it like I do!

In Five Easy Pieces, *Jack Nicholson tried unsuccessfully to order plain toast. Finally, in frustration, he ordered a chicken sandwich on toast, with the following instructions:*

No mayonnaise, no butter . . . and hold the chicken.

*Amateur magician Orson Welles stole the
affection of Rita Hayworth away from Victor
Mature while the three were making a movie.
Mature explained it this way:*

Apparently the way to a girl's heart is to
saw her in half.

*When John Gielgud ordered actors to wear
jockstraps under their leotards, a player
inquired:*

Please, Sir John, does that apply to those of
us who only have small parts?

The title of Anna Karenina *was changed to*
Heat *when it was adapted for the movies.
Screenwriter Frances Marion observed as
follows:*

I think that would be a good ad for Dante's
Inferno, but I'd hate to see on the
billboards: Greta Garbo in Heat!

George Raft was asked where all his movie earnings went. He replied:

Part of the loot went for gambling, part for horses, and part for women. The rest I spent foolishly.

Spencer Tracy described what he wanted in a script:

Days off.

And Tracy's reason for giving Katharine Hepburn second billing was:

This is a movie, not a lifeboat.

The verdict of Fred Astaire's screen test was:

Can't act. Slightly bald. Can dance a little.

During the filming of King's Row, *Ronald Reagan talked politics constantly, resulting in this conversation with Robert Cummings:*

Ronnie, you ought to run for President.
—President of What?
Of the United States.
—Bob, don't you like my acting either?

Greer Garson and a diplomatic photographer had this conversation:

You're not photographing me as well as you used to.
—Well, I'm ten years older.

Fred Astaire, explaining how he danced:

I just put my feet in the air and move them around.

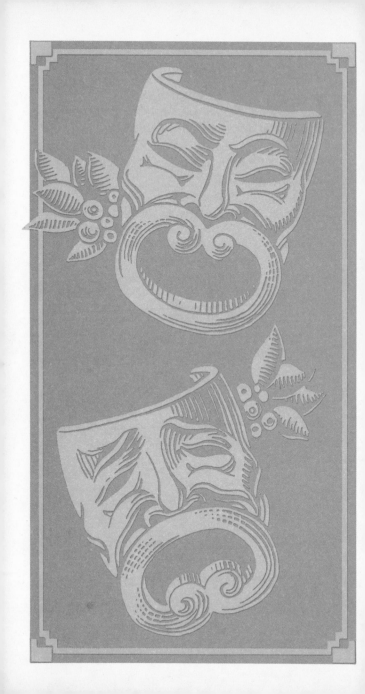

EPITAPHS AND
LAST WORDS

You know what I'm going to have on my
gravestone? "She did it the hard way."

BETTE DAVIS

Yes, Father, I confess to having carnal
thoughts.

JOHN BARRYMORE,
on his deathbed, to a priest

About whom?

PRIEST

About her.

JOHN BARRYMORE,
pointing to the nurse

I picture my epitaph: "Here lies Paul
Newman, who died a failure because his
eyes turned brown."

PAUL NEWMAN

If you want anything, just whistle.
>Inscription on a whistle placed
>with Humphrey Bogart's ashes by
>LAUREN BACALL

This is it. I'm going, I'm going.
>AL JOLSON

I'm looking for a loophole.
>W. C. FIELDS,
>explaining reading a Bible on his deathbed

I would rather be living in Philadelphia.
>W. C. FIELDS,
>suggestion for his own epitaph

I've never felt better.
>DOUGLAS FAIRBANKS,
>last words

Just head for the big star straight on. The highways under it take us right home.
CLARK GABLE,
last movie lines, from *The Misfits*

Don't pull down the blinds! I feel fine. I want the sunlight to greet me.
RUDOLPH VALENTINO

Good night, Mrs. Calabash, wherever you are!
JIMMY DURANTE,
sign-off line,
referring to his late wife

It's tough, isn't it?
GEORGE SEATON,
to Edmund Gwenn, on Gwenn's death bed

Yes it is. But it's not as tough as playing comedy.
EDMUND GWENN

How do you find your way back in the
dark?

MARILYN MONROE

This is too deep for me.

HEDY LAMARR,
her suggestion for her epitaph